ANIMALS
That Make a Difference!

Sharks

Ashley Lee

Explore other books at:
WWW.ENGAGEBOOKS.COM

VANCOUVER, B.C.

℮ WWW.ENGAGEBOOKS.COM

Sharks: Level 1
Animals That Make a Difference!
Lee, Ashley 1995 –
Text © 2021 Engage Books

Edited by: A.R. Roumanis
and Lauren Dick

Text set in Arial Regular.
Chapter headings set in Arial Black.

FIRST EDITION / FIRST PRINTING

LIBRARY AND ARCHIVES CANADA CATALOGUING IN PUBLICATION

Title: Animals That Make a Difference: Sharks Level 1
Names: Lee, Ashley, author.

Identifiers: Canadiana (print) 20200309080 | Canadiana (ebook) 20200309099
ISBN 978-1-77437-667-6 (hardcover)
ISBN 978-1-77437-668-3 (softcover)
ISBN 978-1-77437-669-0 (pdf)
ISBN 978-1-77437-670-6 (epub)
ISBN 978-1-77437-671-3 (kindle)

Subjects:
LCSH: Sharks—Juvenile literature
LCSH: Human-animal relationships—Juvenile literature

Classification: LCC QL638.9 .L44 2020 | DDC J597.3—DC23

Contents

What Are Sharks?

Sharks are a kind of fish.

A group of sharks
is called a school.

What Do Sharks Look Like?

Sharks can be many different sizes. Dwarf lantern sharks are only about 8 inches (20 centimeters) long. Whale sharks can be up to 59 feet (18 meters) long.

Shark teeth are very sharp. Most sharks have between 5 and 15 rows of teeth.

Sharks have a large fin on their backs. This fin helps them keep their balance.

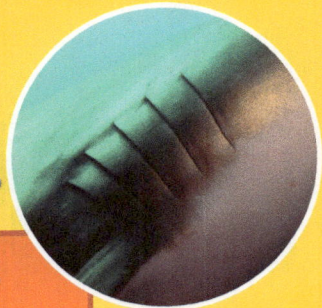

Sharks have holes in their bodies called gills. They use their gills to breathe.

Where Do Sharks Live?

Sharks live in every ocean in the world. Some sharks live in the deepest parts of the ocean. Others live near coral reefs.

Walking sharks are found near Indonesia. Leopard catsharks live near South Africa. Chinese high-fin banded sharks come from the Yangtze River in China.

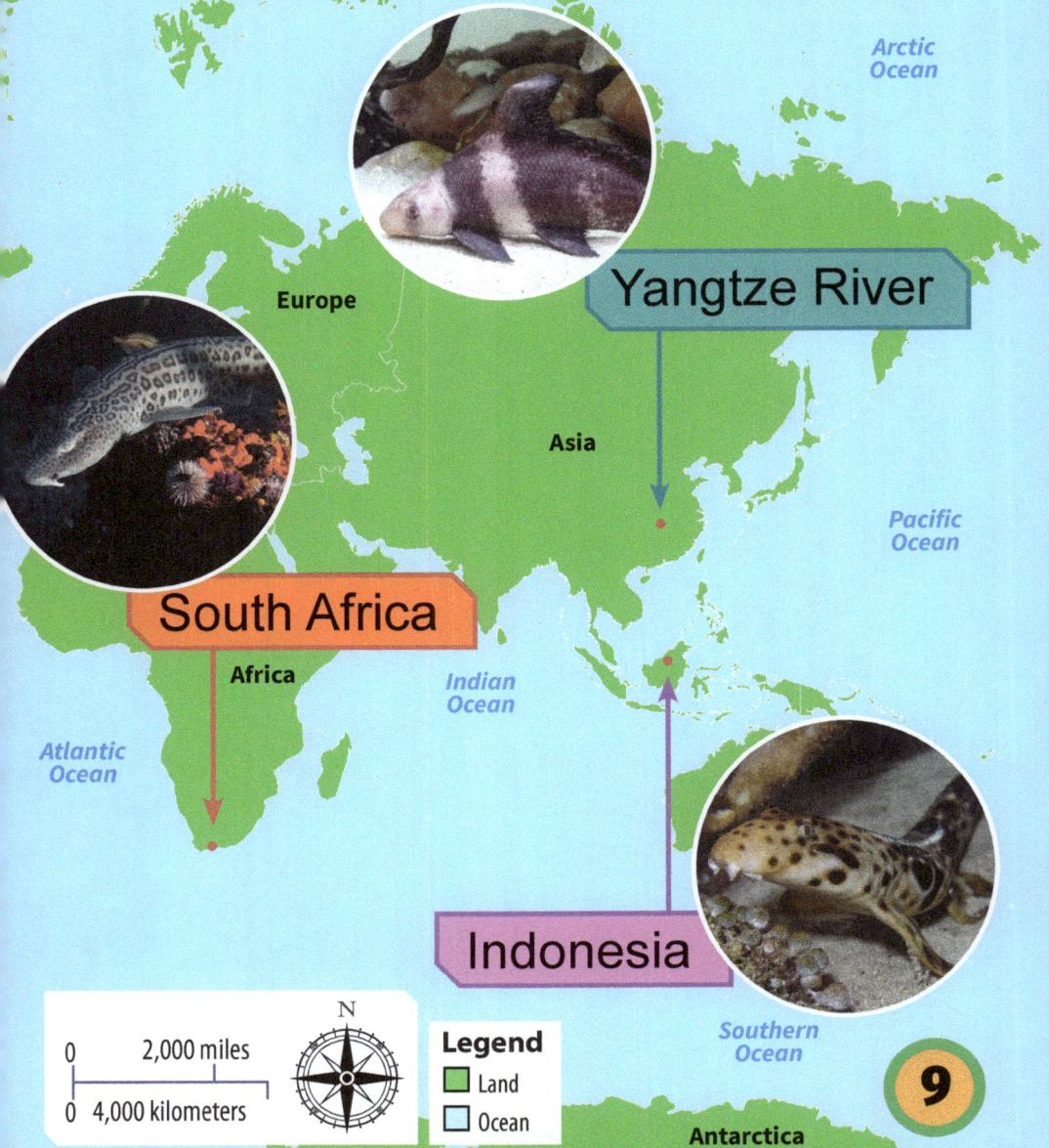

Arctic Ocean

Yangtze River

Europe

Asia

Pacific Ocean

South Africa

Africa

Indian Ocean

Atlantic Ocean

Indonesia

Southern Ocean

0   2,000 miles

0   4,000 kilometers

N

Legend
Land
Ocean

Antarctica

9

What Do Sharks Eat?

Sharks eat other animals that live in the ocean. Small sharks eat fish, squid, and shellfish.

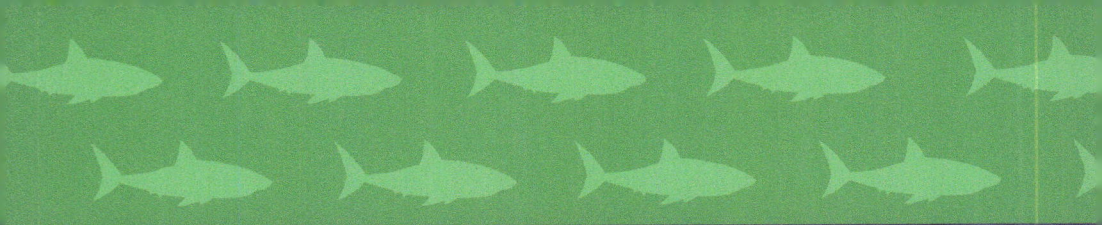

Large sharks eat
dolphins, sea lions,
and sea turtles.

11

How Do Sharks Talk to Each Other?

Sharks move their bodies to tell others how they feel. Different movements mean different things.

Sharks feel vibrations in the water when other animals move. This helps them find other sharks.

Shark Life Cycle

Some sharks lay eggs. Others give birth to live babies.

Most sharks have between 2 and 20 babies. Some sharks can have up to 100 babies.

Baby sharks are called pups. They are able to find food without their mothers.

Scientists have a hard time knowing how old sharks are. They believe some sharks can live for about 400 years.

Curious Facts About Sharks

Whale sharks are the longest fish in the ocean.

Sharks lose about one tooth every week. New teeth grow back in one day.

Sharks lived on Earth before dinosaurs.

A shark's ears are inside its head.

Sharks spend most of their time alone.

Most sharks will sink if they stop swimming. These sharks swim while they sleep.

Kinds of Sharks

There are more than 400 different kinds of sharks. They do not have bones in their bodies. They have a soft material called cartilage. This is the same material found in human ears.

Hammerhead sharks can be gray, brown, or green. They can see behind themselves without turning their heads.

Basking sharks swim with their mouths open. They eat tiny living things called plankton.

Angel sharks have flat bodies. They can blend in with the sea floor so other sharks cannot see them.

How Sharks Help Earth

Sharks make sure ecosystems stay healthy. An ecosystem is an area where living and non-living things live.

Sharks eat green turtles. Green turtles eat seagrass. Without sharks, turtles would eat all the seagrass in an area. Animals that eat seagrass would then disappear. They would have no food.

How Sharks Help Other Animals

Sharks let small fish, called cleaner wrasse fish, clean food out of their teeth.

The sharks do not eat these fish. This gives cleaner wrasse fish lots of food to eat.

How Sharks Help Humans

Sharks do not get sick as often as other animals. Many germs cannot stick to their skin.

Scientists have created a surface that acts like shark skin. Most germs cannot stick to it. This surface is being used in hospitals to help keep people healthy.

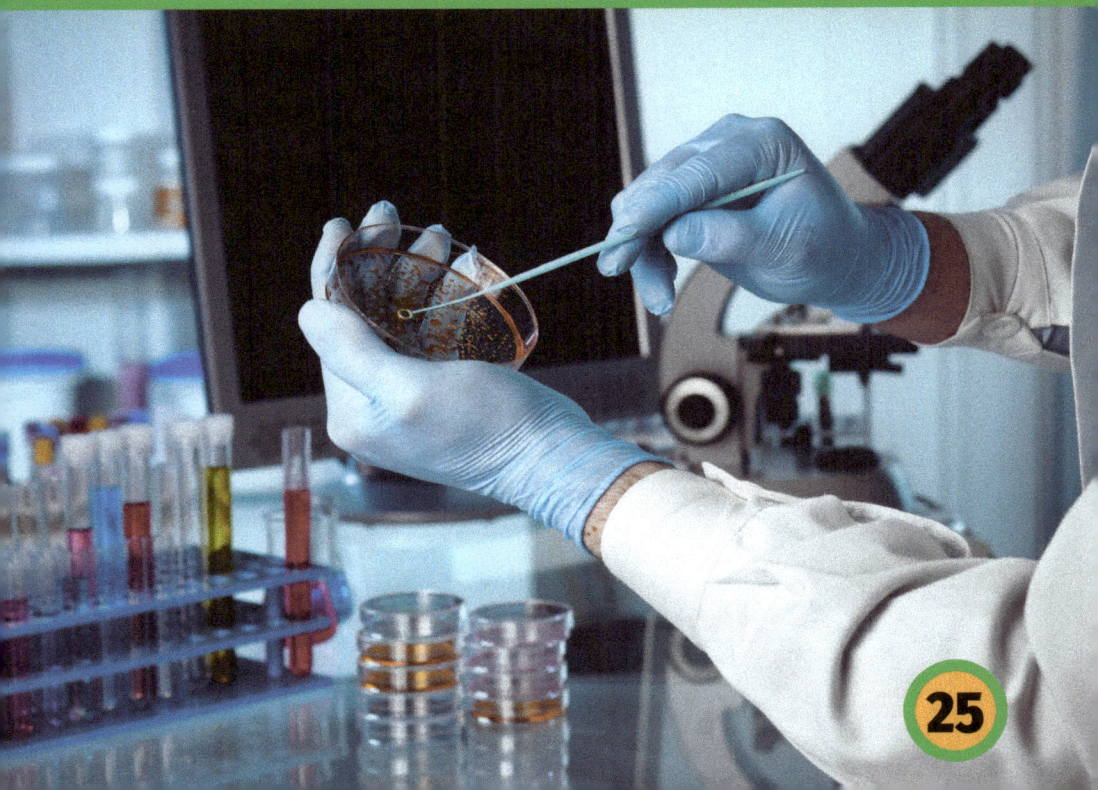

Sharks in Danger

Some people hunt sharks for their fins. They use the fins to make soup. Some shark fins have a chemical in them that can harm humans.

Around 100 million sharks are hunted by humans every year. Most kinds of sharks are in danger of disappearing forever. Many countries have made shark hunting illegal.

How To Help Sharks

Lots of garbage ends up in oceans. Sharks can get trapped in pieces of garbage. They can also get sick if they eat a piece of garbage.

Many people organize ocean clean-ups with their friends and family. This keeps garbage out of oceans and protects sharks.

Quiz

Test your knowledge of sharks by answering the following questions. The questions are based on what you have read in this book. The answers are listed on the bottom of the next page.

1 What is a group of sharks called?

2 What do small sharks eat?

3 What are baby sharks called?

4 How many different kinds of sharks are there?

5 What is an ecosystem?

6 How many sharks are hunted by humans every year?

Explore other books in the Animals That Make a Difference series.

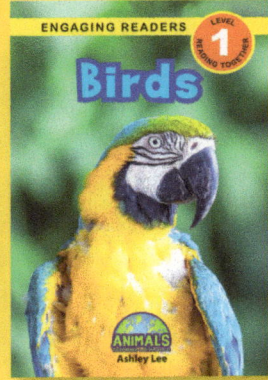

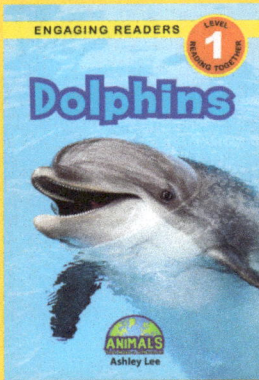

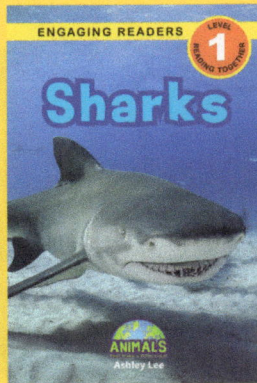

ENGAGING READERS — LEVEL 1 — Bees — Jared Siemens

ENGAGING READERS — LEVEL 1 — Bats — Ashley Lee

ENGAGING READERS — LEVEL 1 — Birds — Ashley Lee

ENGAGING READERS — LEVEL 1 — Dolphins — Ashley Lee

ENGAGING READERS — LEVEL 1 — Horses — Ashley Lee

ENGAGING READERS — LEVEL 1 — Lady Bugs — Ashley Lee

ENGAGING READERS — LEVEL 1 — Pigs — Ashley Lee

ENGAGING READERS — LEVEL 1 — Sharks — Ashley Lee

ENGAGING READERS — LEVEL 1 — Squirrels — Ashley Lee

Visit www.engagebooks.com to explore more Engaging Readers.

Answers: 1. A school 2. Fish, squid, and shellfish 3. Pups 4. More than 400 5. An area where living and non-living things live 6. Around 100 million

www.ingramcontent.com/pod-product-compliance
Lightning Source LLC
Chambersburg PA
CBHW051240020426
42331CB00016B/3455